Centered on Success

About This Book 3

Center Management Checklist 4

Showers for Flowers 5
- 🟡 Sorting letters from other symbols (without numerals)
- 🔵 Sorting letters from other symbols (with numerals)

Letters for Leo 13
- 🟡 Matching letters (uppercase)
- 🔵 Matching letters (uppercase and lowercase)

Duck and Truck 21
- 🟡 Identifying rhyming pictures (four pairs of cards)
- 🔵 Identifying rhyming pictures (six pairs of cards)

Just Like *Mouse* 33
- 🟡 Identifying the beginning sound /m/ (one card without the target sound)
- 🔵 Identifying the beginning sound /m/ (two cards without the target sound)

Just Like *Fish* 41
- 🟡 Identifying the beginning sound /f/ (one card without the target sound)
- 🔵 Identifying the beginning sound /f/ (two cards without the target sound)

Just Like *Turtle* 49
- 🟡 Identifying the beginning sound /t/ (one card without the target sound)
- 🔵 Identifying the beginning sound /t/ (two cards without the target sound)

Just Like *Cat* 57
- 🟡 Identifying the beginning sound /k/ (one card without the target sound)
- 🔵 Identifying the beginning sound /k/ (two cards without the target sound)

Healthy Hare 65
- 🟡 Sequencing a story in three steps (three stories)
- 🔵 Sequencing a story in three steps (four stories)

Brushing Bears 77
- 🟡 Matching uppercase and lowercase letters (six pairs of letters)
- 🔵 Matching uppercase and lowercase letters (12 pairs of letters)

Just Desserts 93
- 🟡 🔵 Matching items one to one

Flashy Findings 101
- 🟡 Copying AB patterns
- 🔵 Copying AAB and ABB patterns

Towering Treats 113
- 🟡 🔵 Ordering by size

Lily Pad Loungers 125
- 🟡 Sorting by color (two different colors)
- 🔵 Sorting by color (three different colors)

Polly's Crackers 137
- 🟡 Sorting by shape (two different shapes)
- 🔵 Sorting by shape (three different shapes)

Up, Up, and Away! 149
- 🟡 Recognizing pictures that illustrate the position word *above*
- 🔵 Recognizing pictures that illustrate the position word *below*

Here a Chick, There a Chick 157
- 🟡 Counting to 5
- 🔵 Identifying numerals, counting to 10

Managing Editor: Kimberly Brugger-Murphy

Editorial Team: Becky S. Andrews, Kimberley Bruck, Karen P. Shelton, Diane Badden, Thad H. McLaurin, Sharon Murphy, Leanne Stratton, Karen A. Brudnak, Sarah Hamblet, Hope Rodgers, Dorothy C. McKinney

Production Team: Lisa K. Pitts, Pam Crane, Rebecca Saunders, Jennifer Tipton Cappoen, Chris Curry, Sarah Foreman, Theresa Lewis Goode, Clint Moore, Greg D. Rieves, Barry Slate, Donna K. Teal, Zane Williard, Tazmen Carlisle, Irene Harvley-Felder, Amy Kirtley-Hill, Kristy Parton, Cathy Edwards Simrell, Lynette Dickerson, Mark Rainey

www.themailbox.com

©2005 The Mailbox®
All rights reserved.
ISBN #1-56234-659-8

Except as provided for herein, no part of this publication may be reproduced or transmitted in any form or by any means, electronic or mechanical, including photocopying, recording, or storing in any information storage and retrieval system or electronic online bulletin board, without prior written permission from The Education Center, Inc. Permission is given to the original purchaser to reproduce patterns and reproducibles for individual classroom use only and not for resale or distribution. Reproduction for an entire school or school system is prohibited. Please direct written inquiries to The Education Center, Inc., P.O. Box 9753, Greensboro, NC 27429-0753. The Education Center®, *The Mailbox*®, the mailbox/post/grass logo, and The Mailbox Book Company® are registered trademarks of The Education Center, Inc. All other brand or product names are trademarks or registered trademarks of their respective companies.

Manufactured in the United States
10 9 8 7 6 5 4 3 2 1

Centered on Success
Preschool

Reinforce essential skills while promoting independent learning with the kid-pleasing center activities in *Centered on Success* for preschool! We've designed 16 all-new center activities to help you reinforce language arts and math skills through appropriately challenging learning experiences. Most centers contain two different skill levels or tasks, so you can match each activity to individual students' needs. For convenience, the two levels are color coded—yellow and blue—for easy identification and management. Simply choose a specific level for each student to complete, or encourage each child through both levels (first yellow, then blue).

Each center contains all the basic materials you need, including full-color, tear-out pages for easy center setup and implementation. Also included for your convenience is a center management checklist on page 4.

Each center includes the following:
- an easy-to-scan teaching page with a skill description for each instructional level, a list of provided materials, simple directions for preparing and using the center, and one or more center options for enhancing or extending the activity
- a full-color center mat, suitable for laminating
- first-level activity cards (yellow)
- second-level activity cards (blue)

Setting up the center:
1. Tear out the perforated pages: teaching page, center mat, and leveled activity cards.
2. Laminate the center mat and activity cards for durability.
3. Cut apart each set of activity cards.
4. Store the cards in resealable plastic bags. Place all center pieces in a large string-tie envelope. Label and store as desired.

Managing the centers:
1. Make a copy of the center checklist on page 4. Program the sheet with students' names and the center titles.
2. Choose a center and decide which level each student will complete. Using a yellow or blue highlighter, mark the appropriate cell on the center checklist to indicate the level each student will complete. Set the checklist aside.
3. Upon each student's completion of the center, assess understanding and mark the center checklist for each child accordingly.

Center Checklist

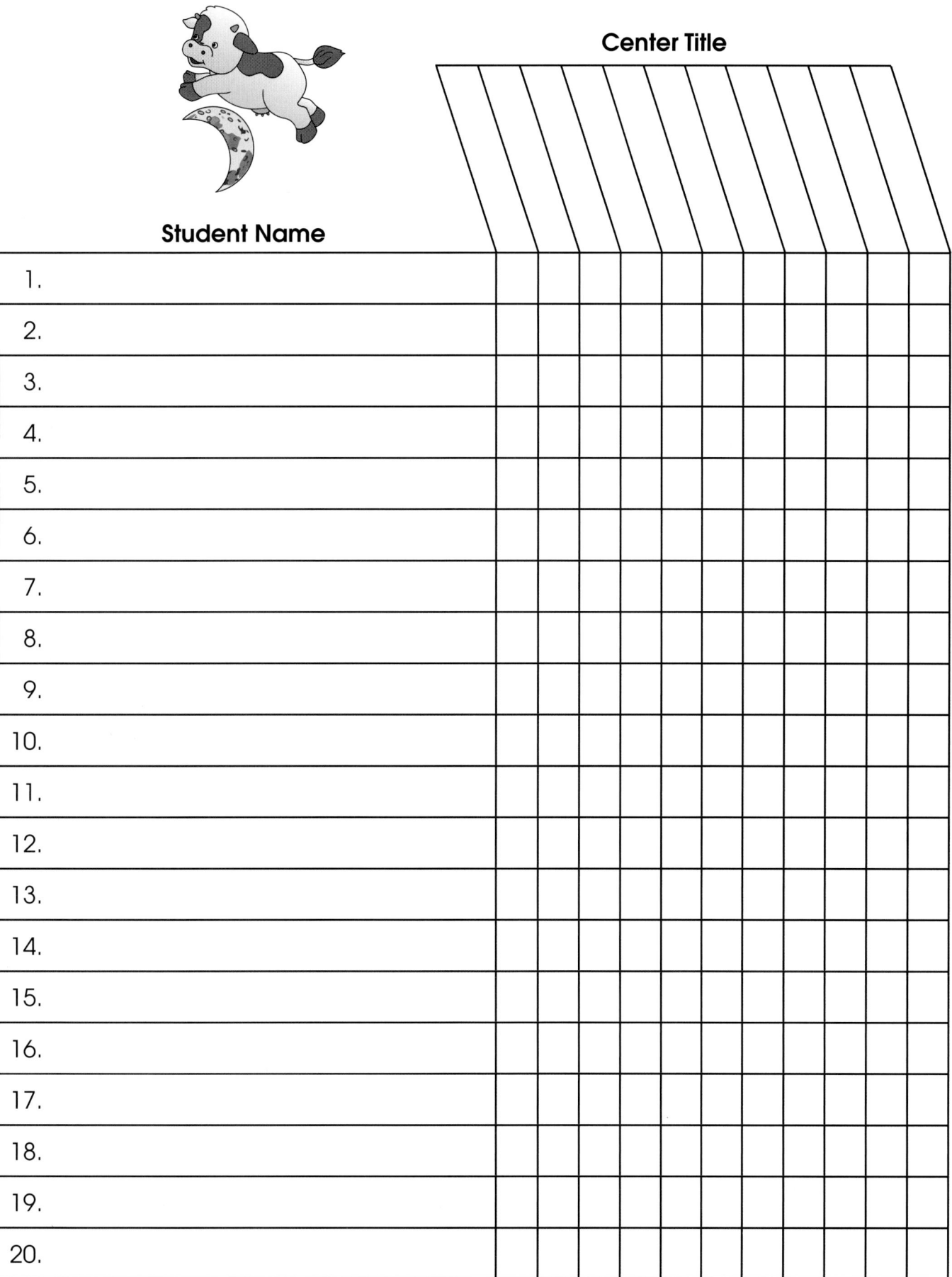

Center Title

Student Name

1.	
2.	
3.	
4.	
5.	
6.	
7.	
8.	
9.	
10.	
11.	
12.	
13.	
14.	
15.	
16.	
17.	
18.	
19.	
20.	

Showers for Flowers

 Sorting letters from other symbols (not including numerals)

 Sorting letters from other symbols (including numerals)

Materials:
- center mat on page 7
- 🟡 activity cards on page 9
- 🔵 activity cards on page 11
- 2 resealable plastic bags

Preparing the centers:
Laminate the center mat and cards if desired. Cut the cards apart and put each set in a separate bag. Then place the bags and center mat at a center.

Using the centers:
1. A child removes the cards from the bag and places each one faceup in the center area.
2. He chooses a card. If the card is labeled with a letter, he places it on the mat. If the card is labeled with a symbol other than a letter, he places it in a separate pile.
3. He repeats Step 2 until each card is sorted.
4. He flips over all the cards on the mat. If each card has a flower on its back, he is finished. If each card does not have a flower, he re-sorts the cards until they are arranged accurately.

For Added Fun

🟡 🔵 Showers for flowers can come from the sky or from a watering can. Place an empty watering can at the center. Each time a child places a card on the mat, encourage him to use the watering can to give the flowers on the mat a pretend shower.

🟡 🔵 Set up the center on a large blue blanket (or on a piece of blue bulletin board paper) to resemble a puddle. Encourage the child to sit on the puddle as he completes the center.

Showers for Flowers

Choose.
Decide.
Place.

Activity Cards
Use with the directions on page 5.

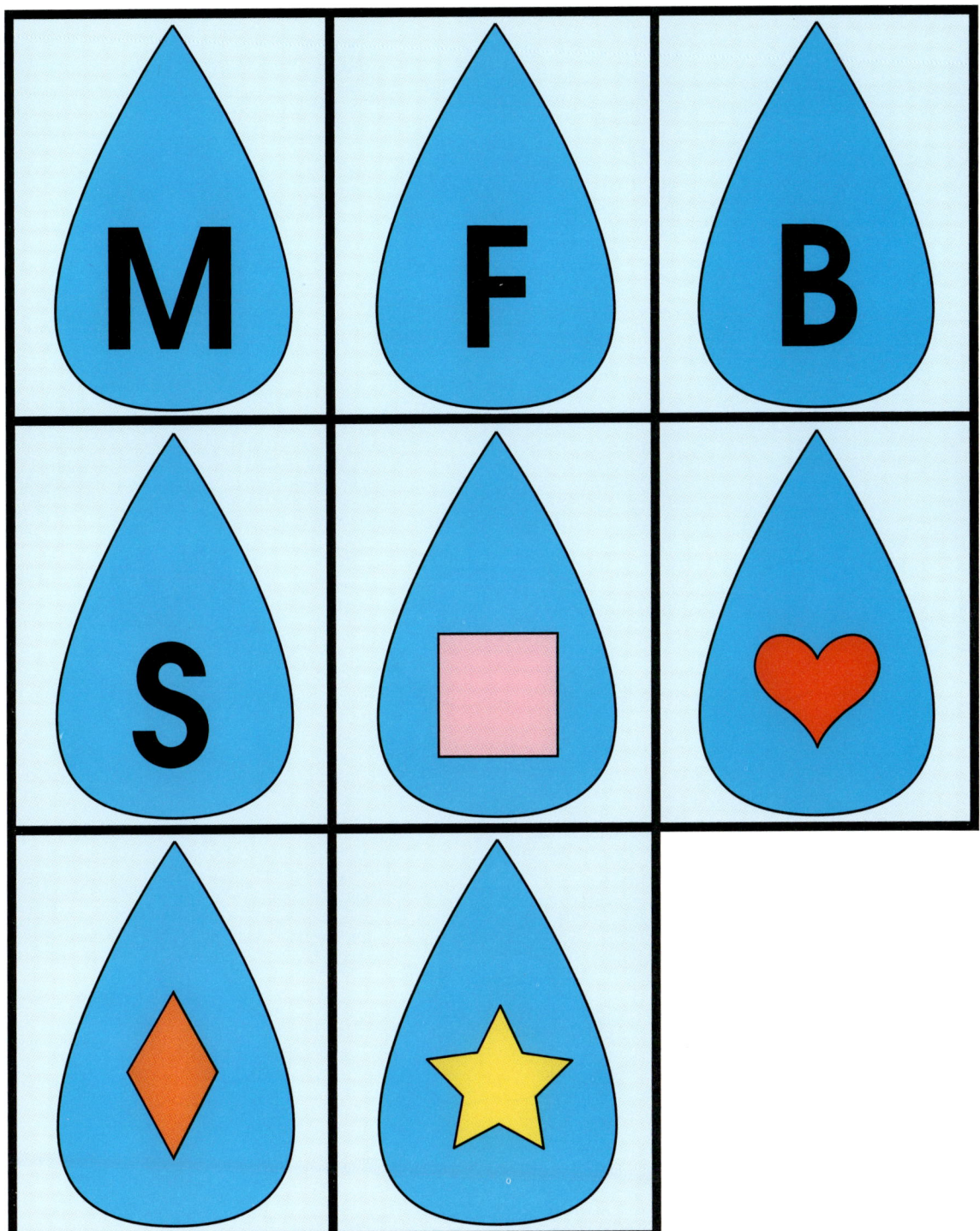

Activity Cards

Use with the directions on page 5.

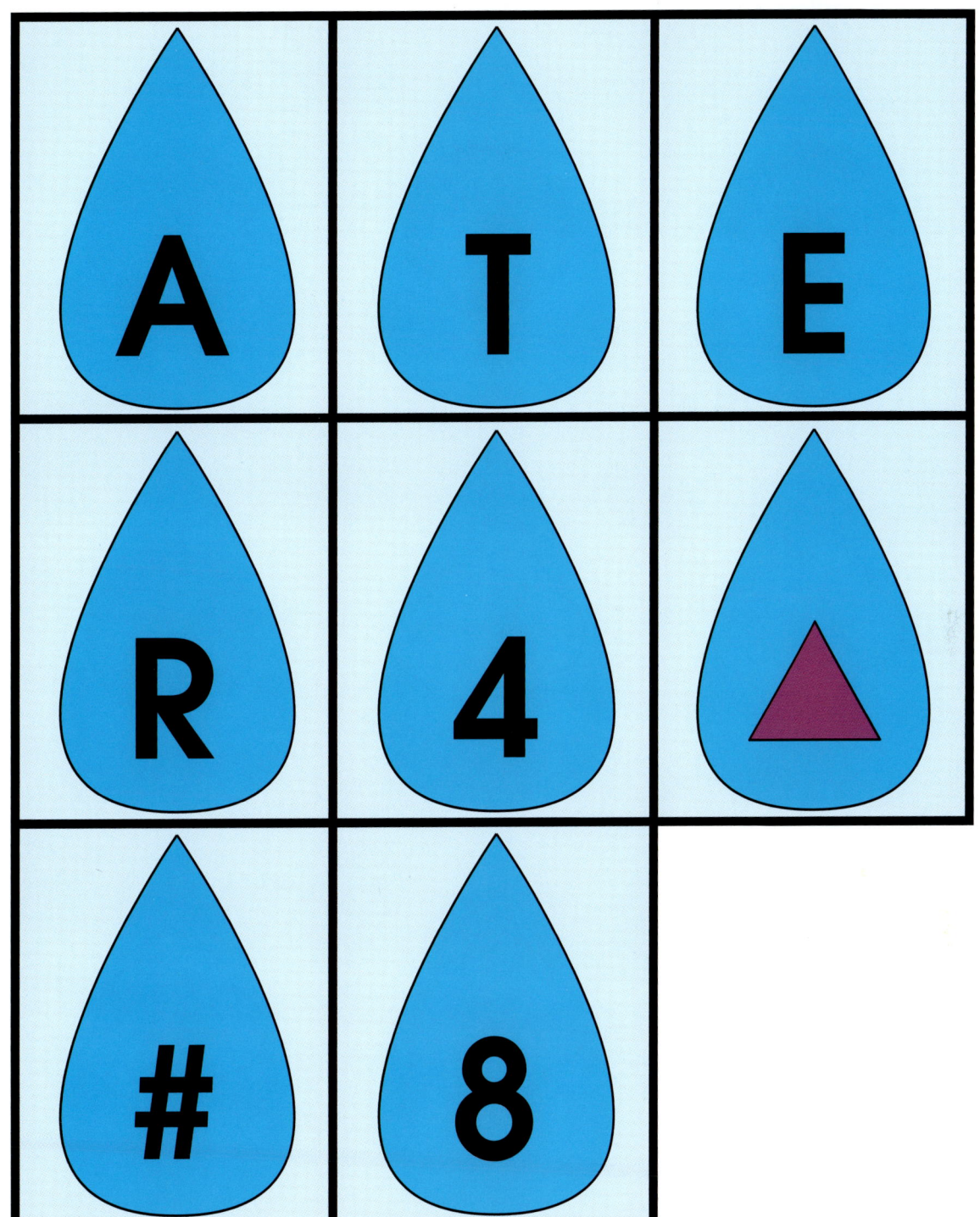

Letters for Leo

 Matching letters (uppercase)

 Matching letters (uppercase and lowercase)

Materials:
- center mat on page 15
- 🟡 activity cards on page 17
- 🔵 activity cards on page 19
- 2 resealable plastic bags

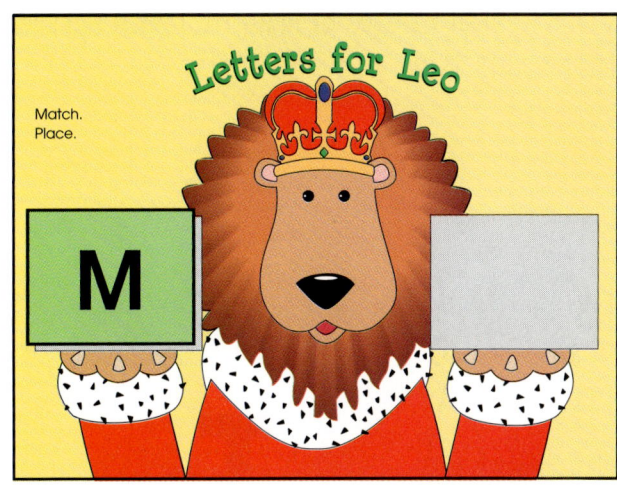

Preparing the centers:
Laminate the center mat and cards if desired. Cut the cards apart and put each set in a separate bag. Then place the bags and center mat at a center.

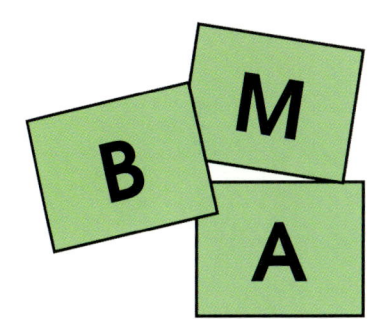

Using the centers:
1. A child removes the cards from the bag and places each one faceup in the center area.
2. He chooses a card and then finds its twin.
3. He flips the cards over to check his answer. If the pictures on the backs of the cards match, he places the cards on the mat. If the pictures do not match, he searches for the correct card to make a matching pair. When he finds the card, he places both cards on the mat.
4. He repeats Steps 2 and 3 until all the cards are placed on the mat.

For Added Fun
🟡 🔵 When a youngster is finished with the center, explain that the lion is sometimes referred to as king of all animals. Staple a strip of scalloped bulletin board border to fit the child's head. Then invite him to wear the resulting crown as a present from Leo the lion for successfully completing the center.

13

Dear Family,
   We have been matching letters. Help your youngster draw a line from each letter on the left to its twin on the right.

Letters for Leo

Match.
Place.

Activity Cards

Use with the directions on page 13.

M	M
B	B
A	A
C	C

Activity Cards

Use with the directions on page 13.

Y	Y
d	d
E	E
g	g

Duck and Truck

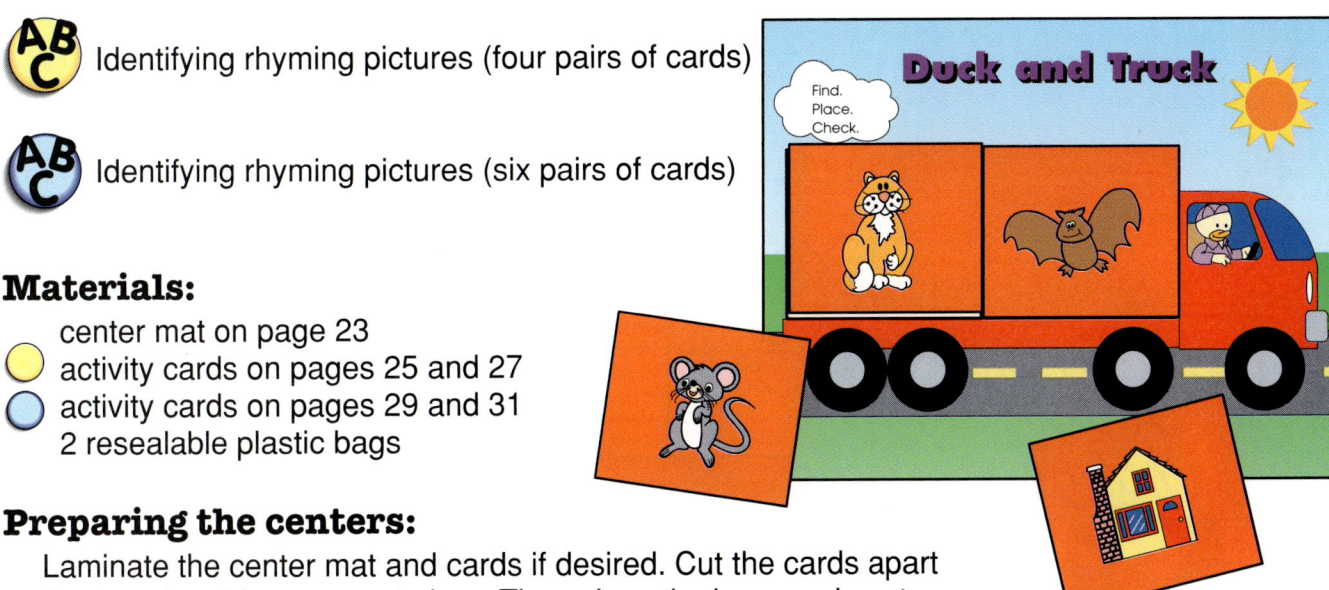

ABC Identifying rhyming pictures (four pairs of cards)

ABC Identifying rhyming pictures (six pairs of cards)

Materials:
- center mat on page 23
- 🟡 activity cards on pages 25 and 27
- 🔵 activity cards on pages 29 and 31
- 2 resealable plastic bags

Preparing the centers:
Laminate the center mat and cards if desired. Cut the cards apart and put each set in a separate bag. Then place the bags and center mat at a center.

Using the centers:
1. A child removes the cards from the bag and places each one faceup in the center area.
2. She chooses a card and names the picture.
3. She finds the card with the rhyming picture.
4. She flips the cards over to check her answer. If the pictures on the backs of the cards match, she places the cards on the mat and proceeds to Step 5. If the pictures do not match, she searches for the correct card. When she finds it, she places both cards on the mat. Then she proceeds to Step 5.
5. She repeats Steps 2–4 until all the cards are placed on the mat.

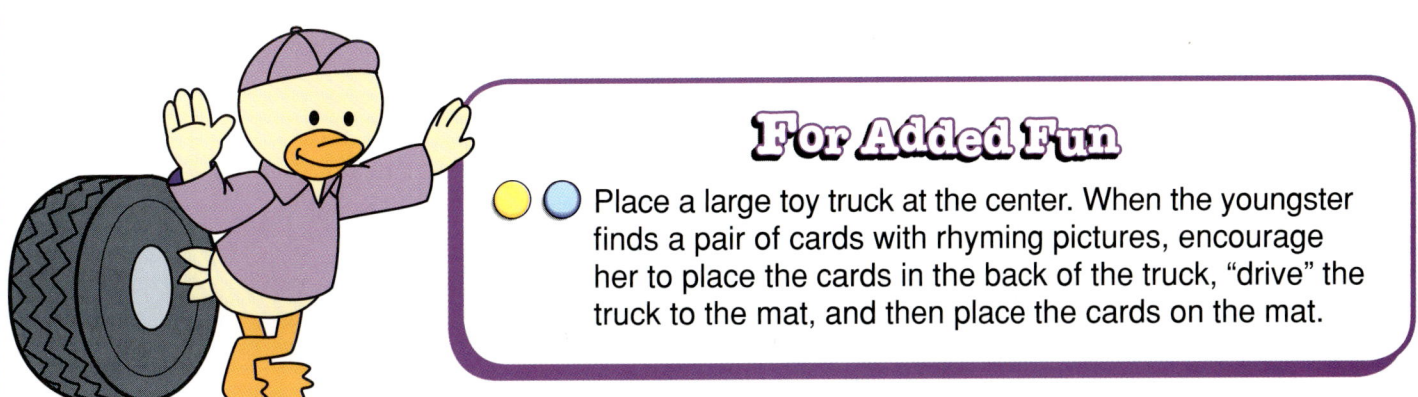

For Added Fun
🟡 🔵 Place a large toy truck at the center. When the youngster finds a pair of cards with rhyming pictures, encourage her to place the cards in the back of the truck, "drive" the truck to the mat, and then place the cards on the mat.

Dear Family,
   We have been matching rhyming pictures. Have your youngster look at the picture on each truck cab and then color the rhyming picture on each truck bed.

Duck and Truck

Find.
Place.
Check.

Activity Cards
Use with the directions on page 21.

Activity Cards
Use with the directions on page 21.

Activity Cards
Use with the directions on page 21.

Activity Cards

Use with the directions on page 21.

Just Like Mouse

 Identifying the beginning sound /m/ (one card without the target sound)

 Identifying the beginning sound /m/ (two cards without the target sound)

Materials:
- center mat on page 35
- activity cards on page 37
- activity cards on page 39
- 2 resealable plastic bags

Preparing the centers:
Laminate the center mat and cards if desired. Cut the cards apart and put each set in a separate bag. Then place the bags and center mat at a center.

Using the centers:
1. A child removes the cards from the bag and places each one faceup in the center area.
2. He chooses a card and names the picture.
3. He decides whether the picture's name begins with /m/ as the word *mouse* does. If it does, he places the card on the mouse's home. If it doesn't, he places it in a separate pile.
4. He repeats Steps 2 and 3 until each card is sorted.
5. He flips all the cards over to check his answers. If each card from the mat has a mouse on its back, he proceeds to Step 6. If each card does not have a mouse, he re-sorts the cards until they are arranged accurately.
6. He removes the stack of cards from the mat and says the name of the picture on each card.

For Added Fun

○ ○ Place at the center a child's toy that makes a squeaking noise when squeezed. Each time the child places a card on the mat, invite him to use the toy to make a squeaking noise to show the mouse's approval!

○ ○ Place a mouse puppet (or stuffed animal) at the center. Have the youngster manipulate the puppet to help him choose each card.

Dear Family,
   We have been listening for the sound of the letter *m*. Help your child say the name of each picture below and decide whether it begins with /m/.

Just Like Mouse

Choose.
Say.
Place.

Activity Cards
Use with the directions on page 33.

Activity Cards

Use with the directions on page 33.

Just Like *Fish*

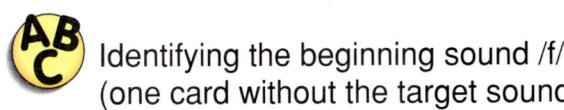 Identifying the beginning sound /f/
(one card without the target sound)

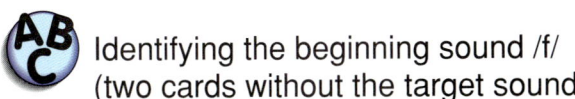 Identifying the beginning sound /f/
(two cards without the target sound)

Materials:
- center mat on page 43
- 🟡 activity cards on page 45
- 🔵 activity cards on page 47
- 2 resealable plastic bags

Preparing the centers:
Laminate the center mat and cards if desired. Cut the cards apart and put each set in a separate bag. Then place the bags and center mat at a center.

Using the centers:
1. A child removes the cards from a bag and places each one faceup in the center area.
2. She chooses a card and names the picture.
3. She decides whether the picture's name begins with /f/ like the sound in the beginning of the word *fish*. If it does, she places the card on the fish. If it doesn't, she places it in a separate pile.
4. She repeats Steps 2 and 3 until each card is sorted.
5. She flips all the cards over to check her answers. If each card from the mat has a fish on the back, she proceeds to Step 6. If not, she re-sorts the cards until they are arranged accurately.
6. She removes the stack of cards from the mat and says the name of the picture on each card.

For Added Fun
🟡 🔵 Label an empty spice container "Fish Food." Place crumpled pieces of colorful tissue paper in the container to resemble fish food, making sure the pieces are too large to fit through the holes. Each time a child places a card on the fish, encourage her to give it a shake of its special food!

Dear Family,
  We have been listening for the sound of the letter *f*. Help your child say the name of the picture on each fish below and decide whether it begins with the /f/ sound.

Activity Cards

Use with the directions on page 41.

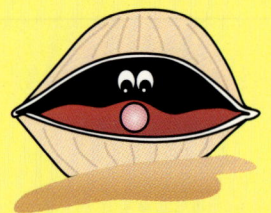

Activity Cards

Use with the directions on page 41.

47

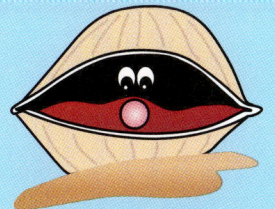
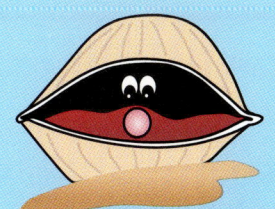

Just Like Turtle

 Identifying the beginning sound /t/
(one card without the target sound)

 Identifying the beginning sound /t/
(two cards without the target sound)

Materials:
- center mat on page 51
- activity cards on page 53
- activity cards on page 55
- 2 resealable plastic bags

Preparing the centers:
Laminate the center mat and cards if desired. Cut the cards apart and put each set in a separate bag. Then place the bags and center mat at a center.

Using the centers:
1. A child removes the cards from the bag and places each one faceup in the center area.
2. He chooses a card and names the picture.
3. He decides whether the picture's name begins with /t/ as the word *turtle* does. If it does, he places the card on the turtle. If it doesn't, he places it in a separate pile.
4. He repeats Steps 2 and 3 until each card is sorted.
5. He flips all of the cards over to check his answers. If each card from the mat has a turtle on the back, he proceeds to Step 6. If not, he re-sorts the cards until they are arranged accurately.
6. He removes the stack of cards from the mat and says the name of the picture on each card.

For Added Fun
Paint an unsharpened pencil (or a short dowel rod) green. After the paint is dry, glue a brown construction paper oval to the pencil to transform it into a cattail. When the youngster reaches Step 6 above, have him remove the stacked cards from the mat and place them in a row. Then encourage him to use the cattail as a pointer as he names the picture on each card.

Dear Family,
   We have been listening for the sound of the letter *t*. Help your child say the name of each picture on the turtle and decide whether it begins with the /t/ sound.

Just Like Cat

 Identifying the beginning sound /k/
(one card without the target sound)

 Identifying the beginning sound /k/
(two cards without the target sound)

Materials:
- center mat on page 59
- activity cards on page 61
- activity cards on page 63
- 2 resealable plastic bags

Preparing the centers:
Laminate the center mat and cards if desired. Cut the cards apart and put each set in a separate bag. Then place the bags and center mat at a center.

Using the centers:
1. A child removes the cards from the bag and places each one faceup in the center area.
2. He chooses a card and names the picture.
3. He decides whether the picture's name begins with /k/ like the beginning sound in the word *cat.* If it does, he places the card on the cat. If it doesn't, he places it in a separate pile.
4. He repeats Steps 2 and 3 above until each card is sorted.
5. He flips all of the cards over to check his answers. If each card from the mat has a picture of a cat on the back, he proceeds to Step 6. If not, he re-sorts the cards until they are arranged accurately; then he proceeds to Step 6.
6. He removes the stack of cards from the mat and says the name of the picture on each card.

For Added Fun

Have a youngster complete the center as described above. Prompt the child to notice the cat and the caterpillar on the mat. Then explain that both the word *cat* and the word *caterpillar* begin with /k/. Give the child two short lengths of chenille stem in two different shades of green and encourage him to twist the lengths together to make his very own caterpillar to take home!

Dear Family,
  We have been listening for the /k/ sound of the letter c. Help your child say the name of each picture below and decide whether it begins with the /k/ sound.

Just Like Cat

Choose.
Say.
Place.

59

Activity Cards

Use with the directions on page 57.

Activity Cards

Use with the directions on page 57.

Healthy Hare

 Sequencing a story in three steps (three stories)

 Sequencing a story in three steps (four stories)

Materials:
- center mat on page 67
- 🟡 activity cards on pages 69 and 71
- 🔵 activity cards on pages 73 and 75
- 7 resealable plastic bags

Preparing the centers:
Laminate the center mat and cards if desired. Cut the cards apart. Then put the cards for each story in a separate bag. Place the bags and center mat at a center.

Using the centers:
1. A child removes the cards from a bag and places each card faceup in the center area.
2. He places the cards in order on the mat to show the correct sequence of events.
3. He flips the cards over to check his answer. If the cards are in the correct order, he places them back in the bag. If the cards are not in the correct order, he reorders them until they are arranged correctly; then he places the cards in the bag.
4. He repeats Steps 1–3 for each bag of cards.

For Added Fun
🟡 🔵 If the cards and mat are not laminated, laminate them before using this section. Place a small container of bubbles and a bubble wand at the center. After the youngster correctly orders a set of cards, invite him to blow several bubbles to add to Hare's bubbly bath time.

Dear Family,
We have been sequencing the events in a story. Help your child cut out the cards below. Then encourage your youngster to place each set of cards in order to show the sequence of events.

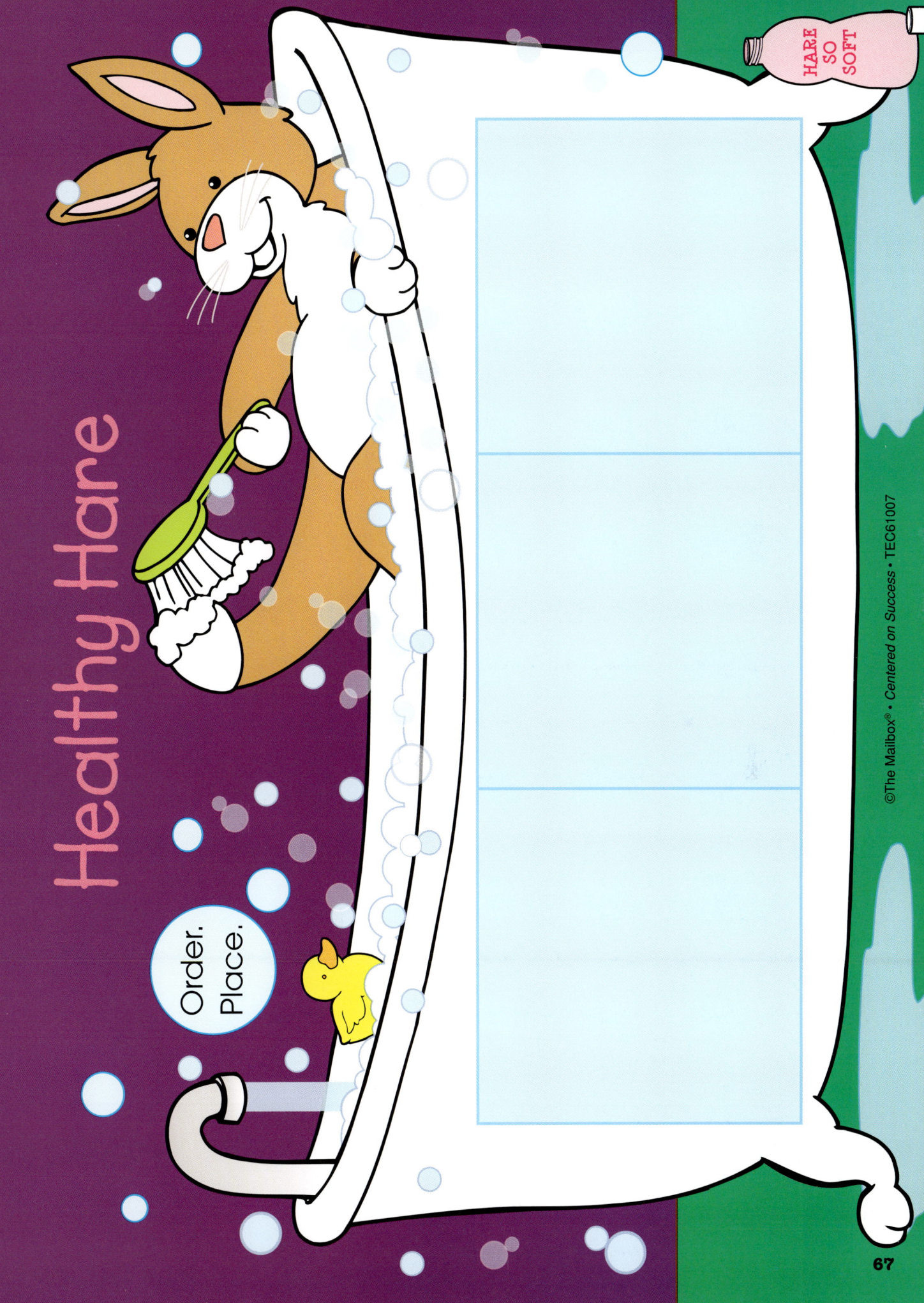

Activity Cards

Use with the directions on page 65.

1   1

2   2

3   3

Activity Cards
Use with the directions on page 65.

1

2

3

Activity Cards

Use with the directions on page 65.

1   1

2   2

3   3

Activity Cards
Use with the directions on page 65.

1	1
2	2
3	3

Brushing Bears

 Matching uppercase and lowercase letters (six pairs of letters)

 Matching uppercase and lowercase letters (12 pairs of letters)

Materials:
- center mat on page 79
- activity cards on pages 81 and 83
- activity cards on pages 85, 87, 89, and 91
- 2 resealable plastic bags

Preparing the centers:
Laminate the center mat and cards if desired. Cut the cards apart and put each set in a separate bag. Then place the bags and center mat at a center.

Using the centers:
1. A child removes the cards from a bag and places each one faceup in the center area.
2. She chooses an uppercase letter and then finds the matching lowercase letter.
3. She flips the cards over. If the backs of the cards have matching pictures, she places the cards on the mat. If the pictures do not match, she finds the correct lowercase letter card; then she places the cards on the mat.
4. She repeats Steps 2 and 3 until all the cards are placed on the mat.

For Added Fun
Place a small paintbrush at the center. Before the youngster places each card on the mat, encourage her to say the letter's name as she traces it with the dry paintbrush.

Dear Family,
   We have been matching uppercase and lowercase letters. Help your child draw a line from each uppercase letter on the left side of the paper to the corresponding lowercase letter on the right side of the paper.

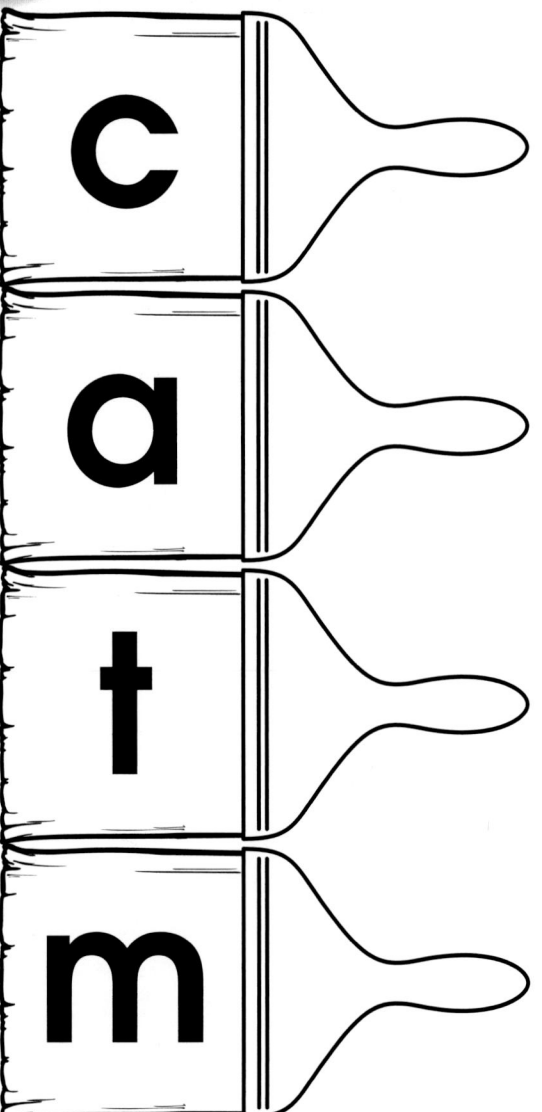

Brushing Bears

Match.
Check.
Place.

Activity Cards
Use with the directions on page 77.

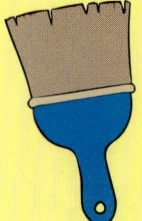
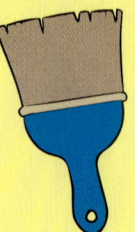
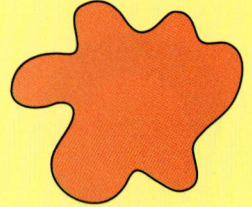
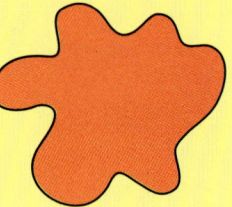

Activity Cards
Use with the directions on page 77.

S	s
F	f
P	p

Activity Cards
Use with the directions on page 77.

Activity Cards
Use with the directions on page 77.

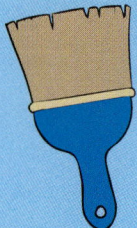

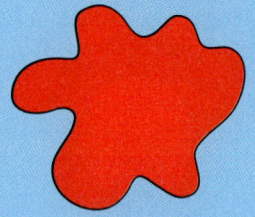
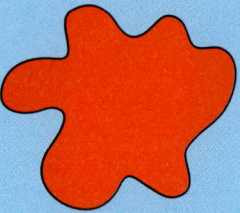

Activity Cards
Use with the directions on page 77.

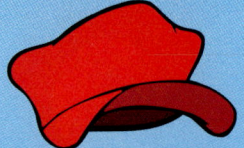 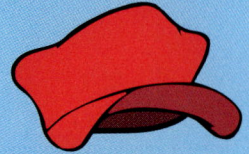

Activity Cards
Use with the directions on page 77.

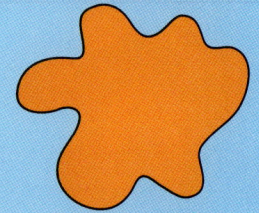

Just Desserts

 Matching items one to one

Materials:
- center mat on page 95
- activity cards on page 97
- activity cards on page 99
- 2 resealable plastic bags

Preparing the centers:
Laminate the center mat and cards if desired. Cut the cards apart and put each set in a separate bag. Then place the bags and center mat at a center.

Using the centers:
1. A child removes the cards from the bag and places each one faceup in the center area.
2. He counts the number of plates on the mat and then counts the number of cards.
3. He chooses a card and places it above a plate on the mat.
4. He repeats Step 3 until each card is placed above a different plate.

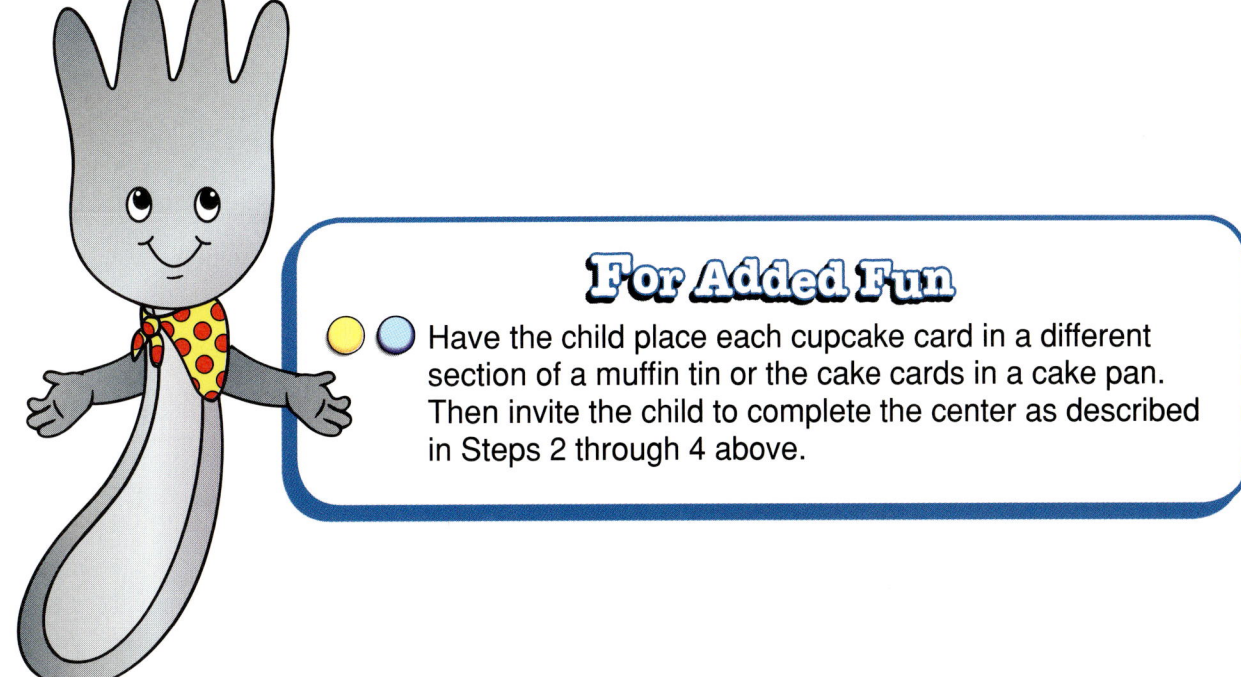

For Added Fun
Have the child place each cupcake card in a different section of a muffin tin or the cake cards in a cake pan. Then invite the child to complete the center as described in Steps 2 through 4 above.

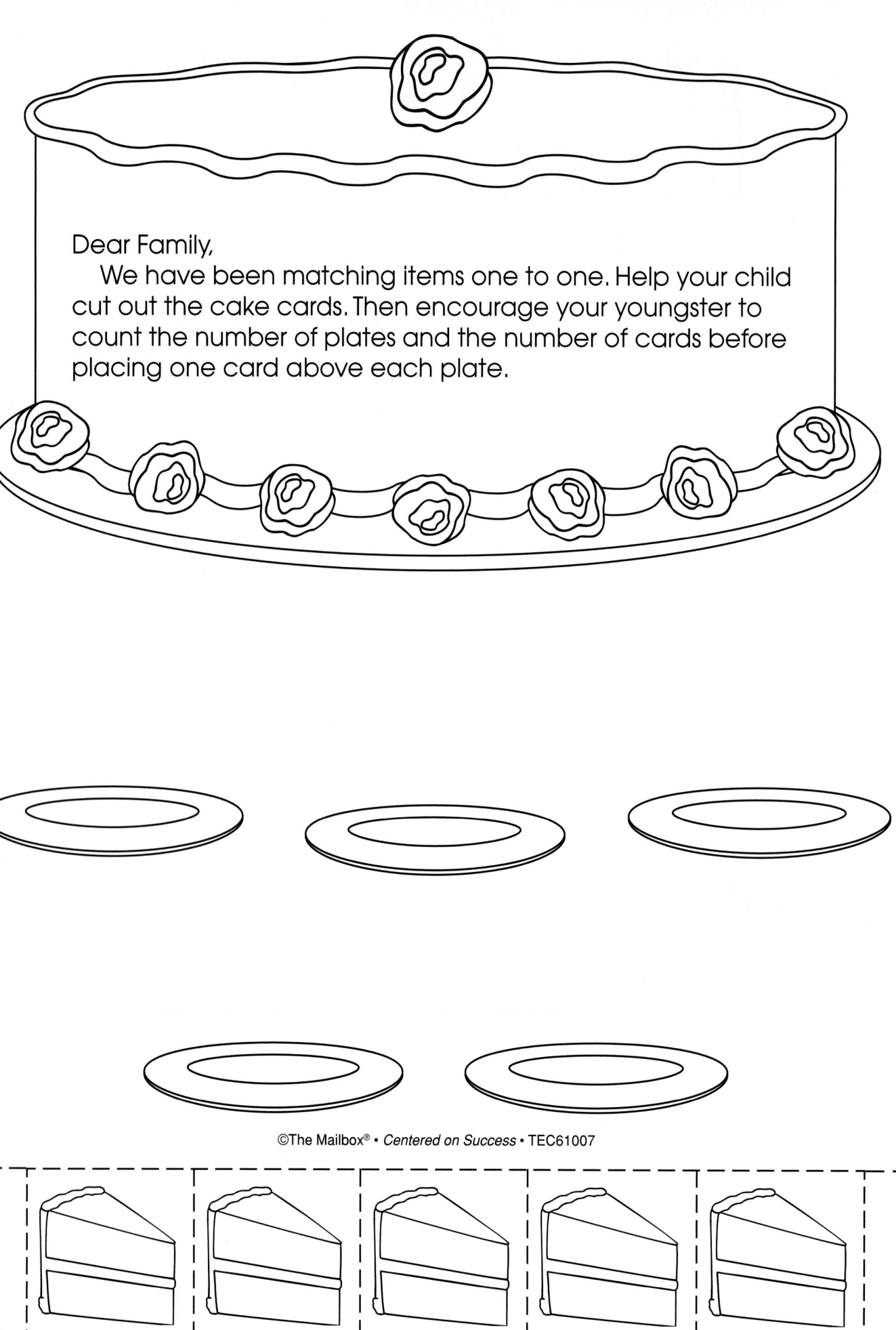

Just Desserts

Choose.
Place.

Activity Cards
Use with the directions on page 93.

Activity Cards
Use with the directions on page 93.

Flashy Findings

 Copying AB patterns

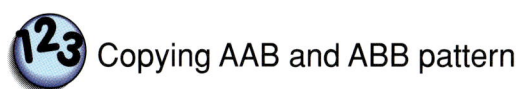 Copying AAB and ABB patterns

Materials:
- center mat on page 103
- activity strips and cards on pages 105 and 107
- activity strips and cards on pages 109 and 111
- 2 large resealable plastic bags

Preparing the centers:
Laminate the center mat, strips, and cards if desired. Cut the strips and cards apart and put each set in a separate bag. Then place the bags and center mat at a center.

Using the centers:
1. A child removes the strips and cards from a bag. She places each card faceup in the center area. She places a strip on the mat.
2. She reads the pattern, naming the colors of the jewels from left to right as she points to each one.
3. She duplicates the pattern by placing matching cards below the strip.
4. She repeats Steps 2 and 3 for each remaining strip.

For Added Fun

Place a supply of flashy costume jewelry in a box (treasure chest). Place the treasure chest at the center. Encourage the youngster to dress up with jewels from the treasure chest. Then have her complete the center as directed above. When she's finished, have her place the jewels back in the treasure chest for the next child.

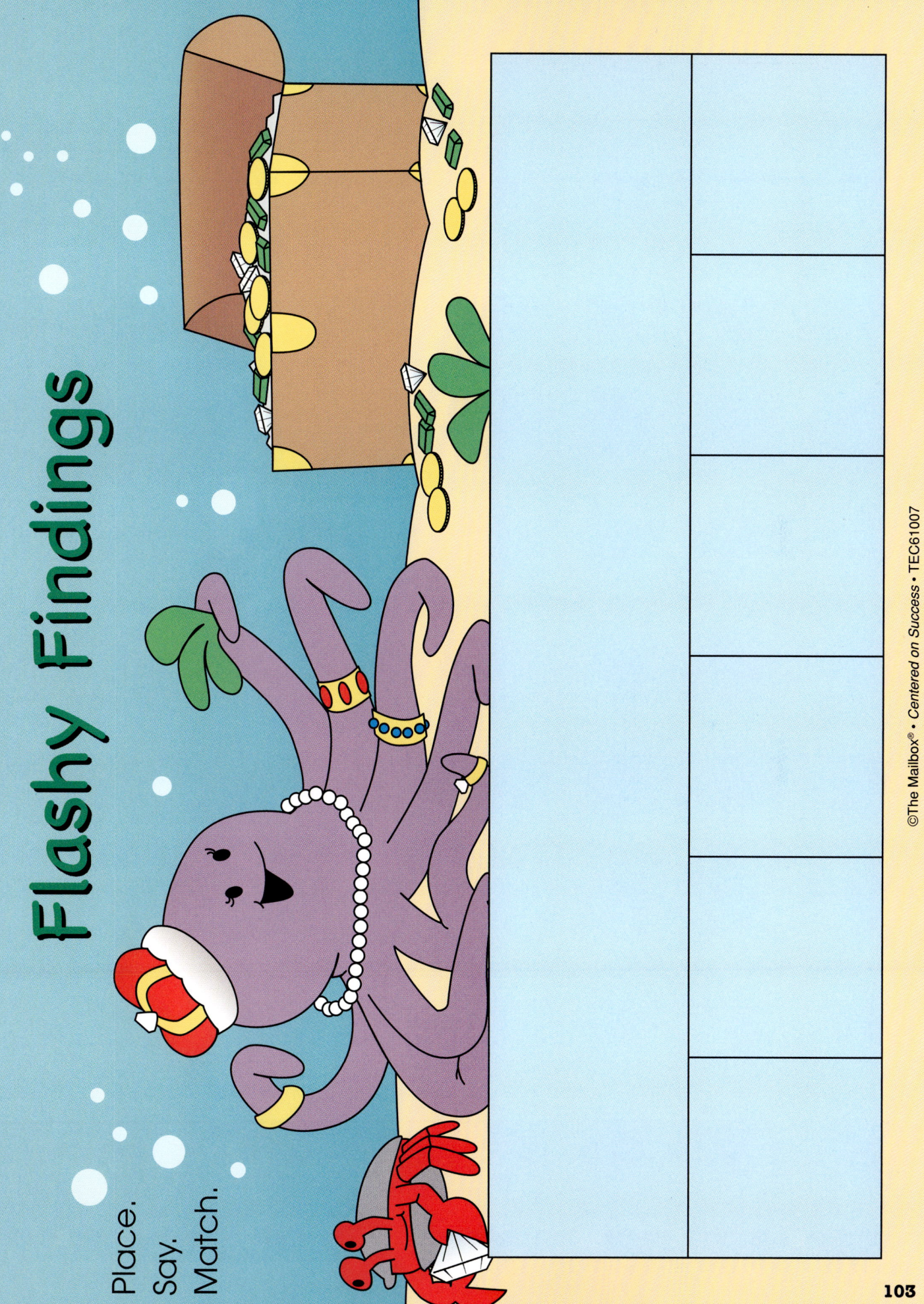

Activity Strips and Cards
Use with the directions on page 101.

106

Activity Strips and Cards
Use with the directions on page 101.

Activity Strips and Cards

Use with the directions on page 101.

Activity Strips and Cards
Use with the directions on page 101.

Towering Treats

 Ordering by size

Materials:
- center mat on page 115
- activity cards on pages 117 and 119
- activity cards on pages 121 and 123
- 2 resealable plastic bags

Preparing the centers:
Laminate the center mat and cards if desired. Cut the cards apart and put each set in a separate bag. Then place the bags and center mat at a center.

Using the centers:
1. A child removes the cards from the bag and places each one faceup in the center area.
2. He chooses the cards for one type of treat. Then he arranges them in order by size on the center mat.
3. He flips all of the cards over to check his answers. If the numbers on the backs of the cards are in order, he places the cards in the bag. If the numbers aren't in order, he rearranges the cards until they are in the correct order; then he places the cards in the bag.
4. He repeats Steps 2 and 3 for the remaining set of cards.

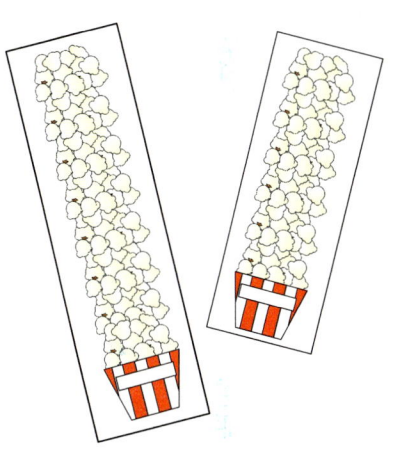

For Added Fun
 Place ice-cream scoops and plastic bowls at your play dough center. After a youngster completes the ordering center, invite him to visit the play dough center to design his own towering treat.

113

Dear Family,
   We have been ordering pictures by size. Help your child cut out the cards below and then place them in a row from shortest to tallest.

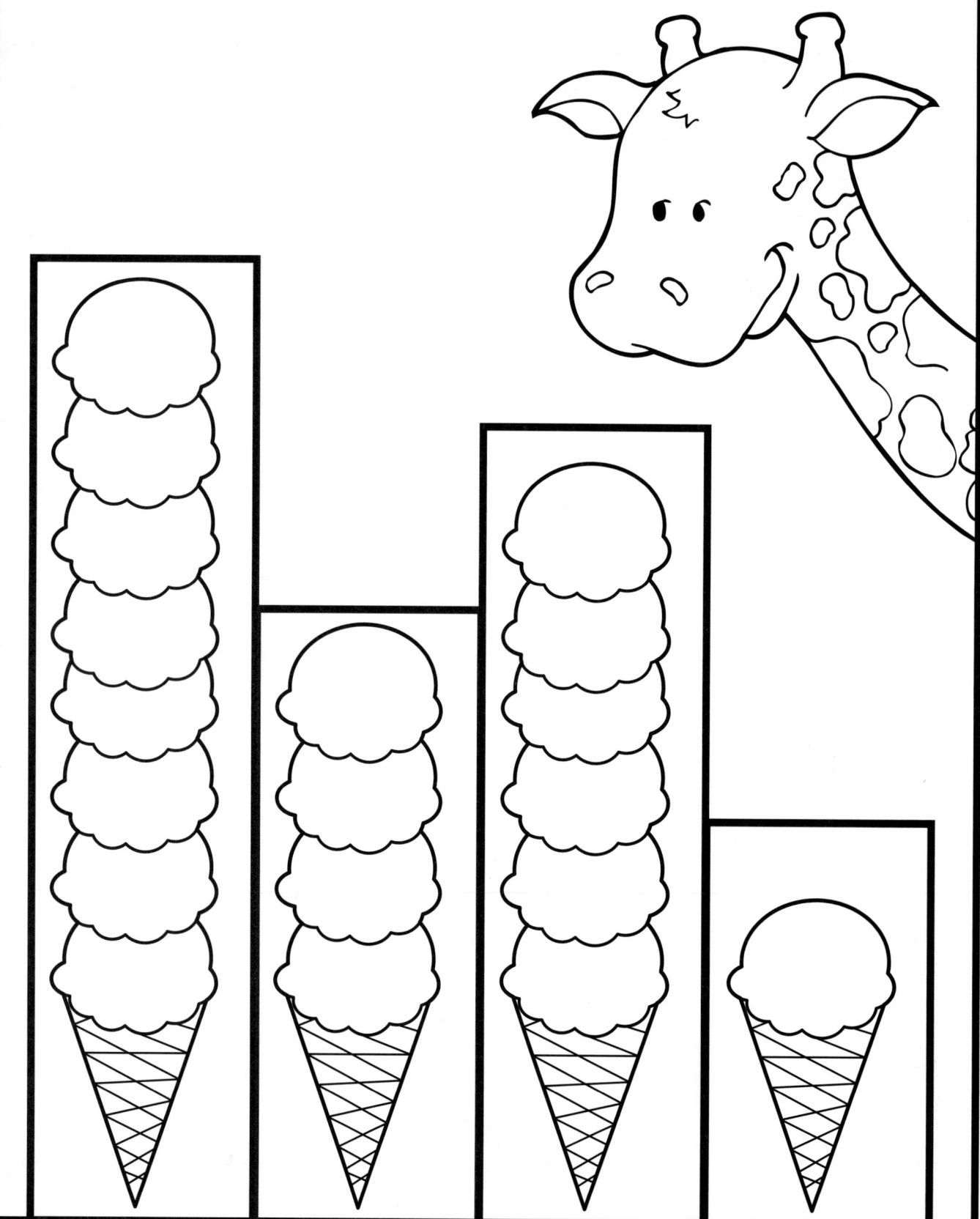

114 ©The Mailbox® • *Centered on Success* • TEC61007

Towering Treats

Place.

115

Activity Cards
Use with the directions on page 113.

4

3

2

1

Activity Cards

Use with the directions on page 113.

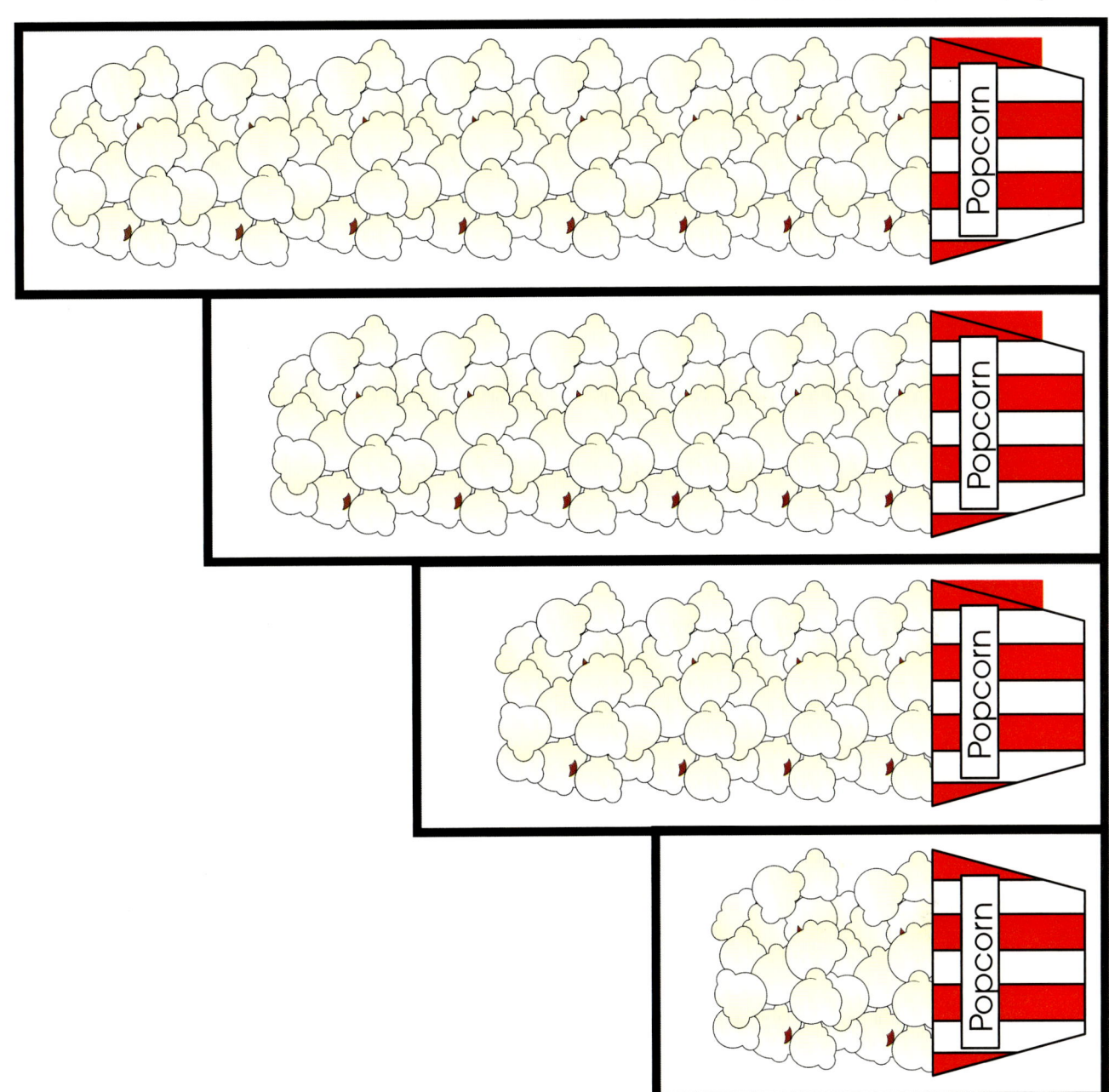

4

3

2

1

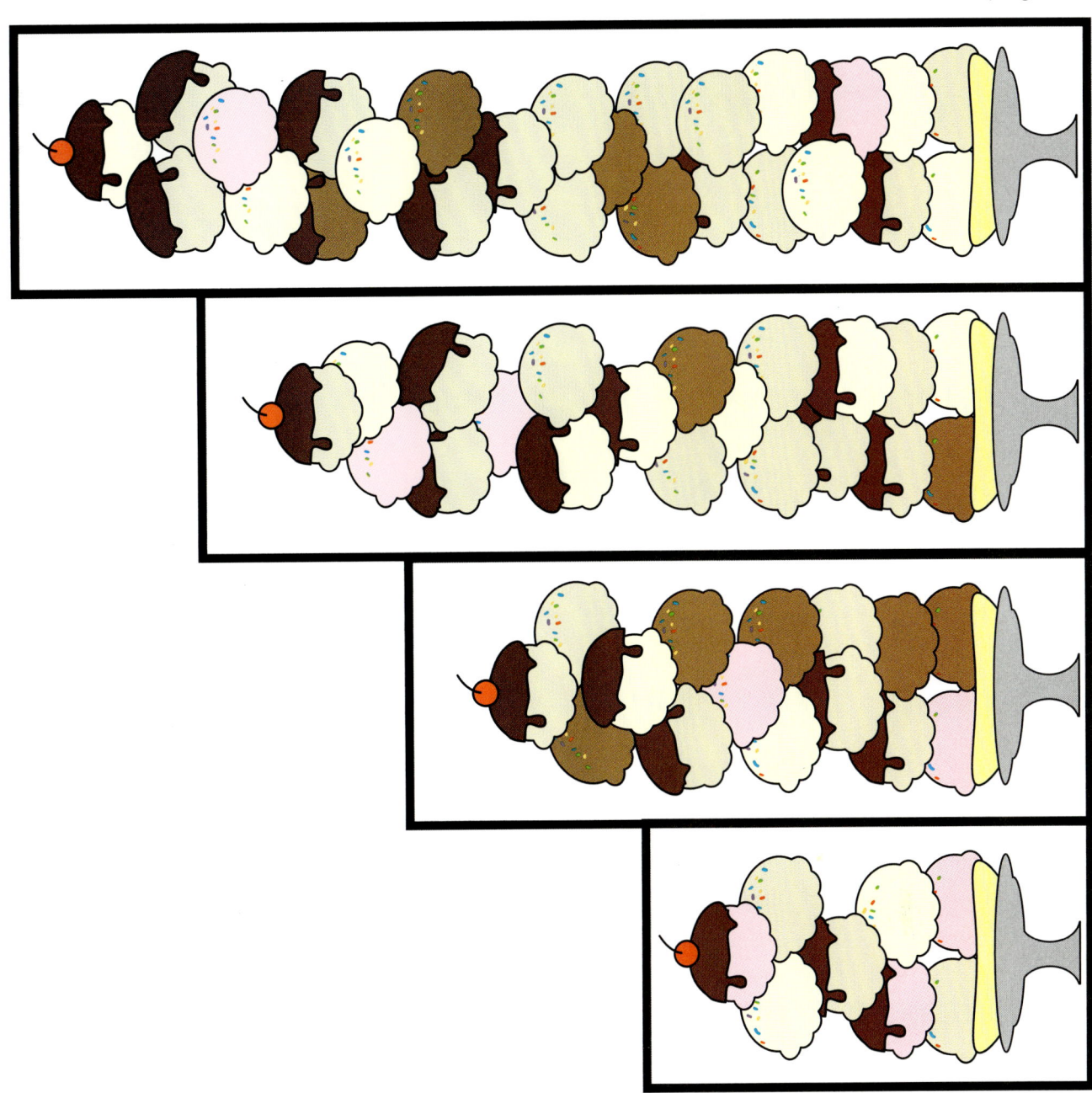

Activity Cards
Use with the directions on page 113.

121

4

3

2

1

Activity Cards
Use with the directions on page 113.

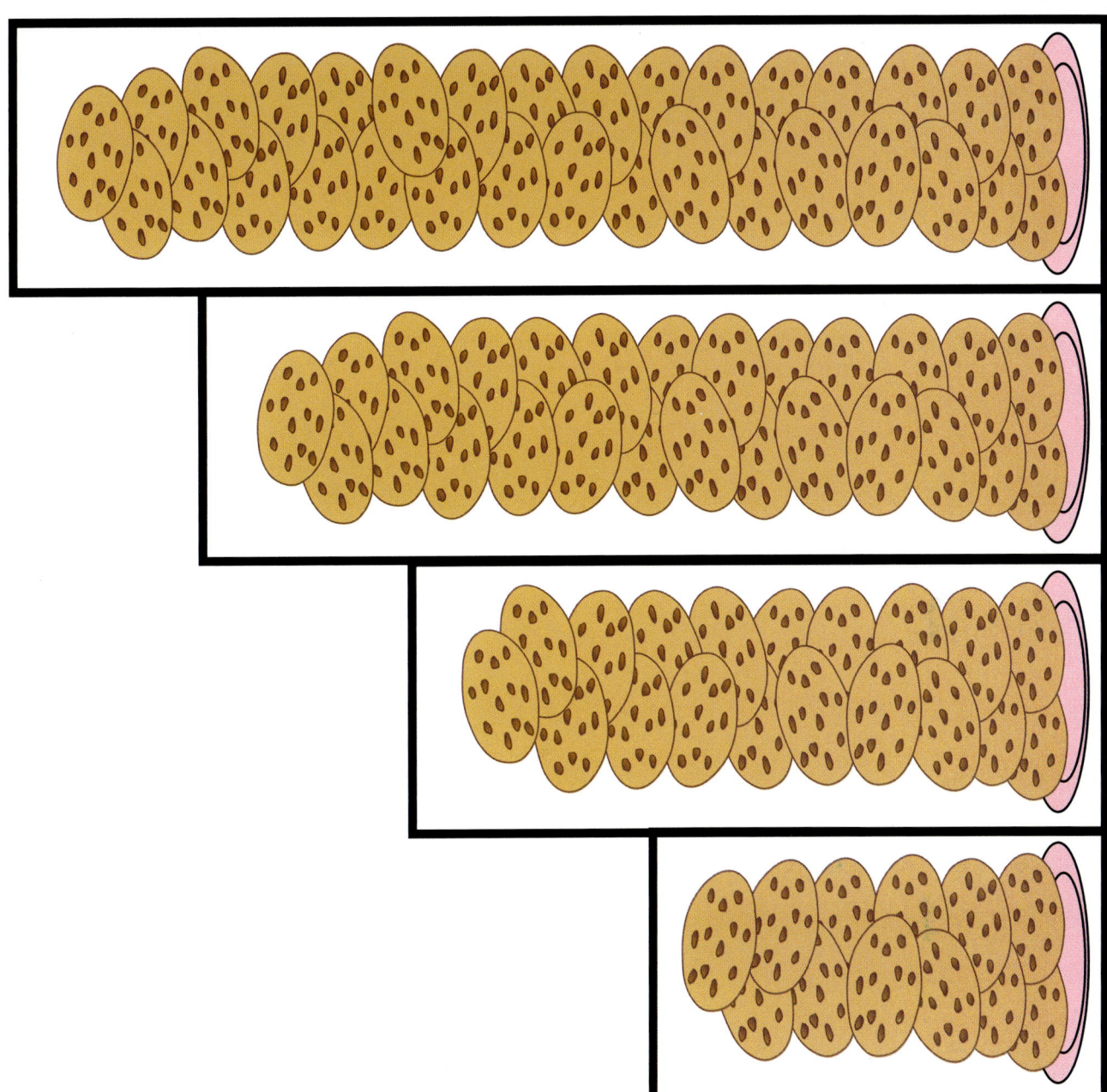

4

3

2

1

Lily Pad Loungers

 Sorting by color (two different colors)

 Sorting by color (three different colors)

Materials:
- center mat on page 127
- 🟡 activity cards on pages 129 and 131
- 🔵 activity cards on pages 133 and 135
- 2 resealable plastic bags

Preparing the centers:
Laminate the center mat and cards if desired. Cut the cards apart and put each set in a separate bag. Then place the bags and center mat at a center.

Using the centers:
1. A child removes the cards from the bag and places each one faceup in the center area.
2. She chooses a card, looks at the frog's clothing, and places the card on the lily pad with the corresponding flower color.
3. She repeats Step 2 with each remaining card.
4. She removes each pile of cards from its lily pad and then flips the cards over to check her answers. If the cards from each pile have matching pictures, she is finished. If they do not have matching pictures, she rearranges the cards until they are sorted correctly.

For Added Fun

🟡 🔵 Make a log from a piece of construction paper. Place the frog cards on the log a few feet away from the mat. Encourage the child to choose a frog card from the log and make it "hop" to the mat and land on its matching lily pad. Have her repeat the process for each card on the log.

Dear Family,
We have been sorting by color. Encourage your child to color three cards blue and three cards red. Then help your youngster cut out the cards and sort them into two piles according to color.

Activity Cards

Use with the directions on page 125.

Activity Cards

Use with the directions on page 125.

◯ **Activity Cards**
Use with the directions on page 125.

©The Mailbox® • *Centered on Success* • TEC61007

Activity Cards
Use with the directions on page 125.

Polly's Crackers

 Sorting by shape (two different shapes)

 Sorting by shape (three different shapes)

Materials:
- center mat on page 139
- 🟡 activity cards on pages 141 and 143
- 🔵 activity cards on pages 145 and 147
- 2 resealable plastic bags

Preparing the centers:
Laminate the center mat and cards if desired. Cut the cards apart and put each set in a separate bag. Then place the bags and center mat at a center.

Using the centers:
1. A child removes the cards from the bag and places each one faceup in the center area.
2. He chooses a card and places it on the cracker box labeled with the corresponding shape.
3. He repeats Step 2 with each card.
4. He removes each pile of cards and then flips the cards over to check his answers. If the cards from each pile have matching pictures, he is finished. If they do not have matching pictures, he rearranges the cards until they are sorted correctly.

For Added Fun
🟡 🔵 After the child has completed the center, explain that Polly the parrot has decided to share some of her crackers. Give the youngster a plate with several crackers in the following shapes: squares, triangles, and circles. Encourage him to sort the crackers according to shape. Then invite him to nibble on his snack.

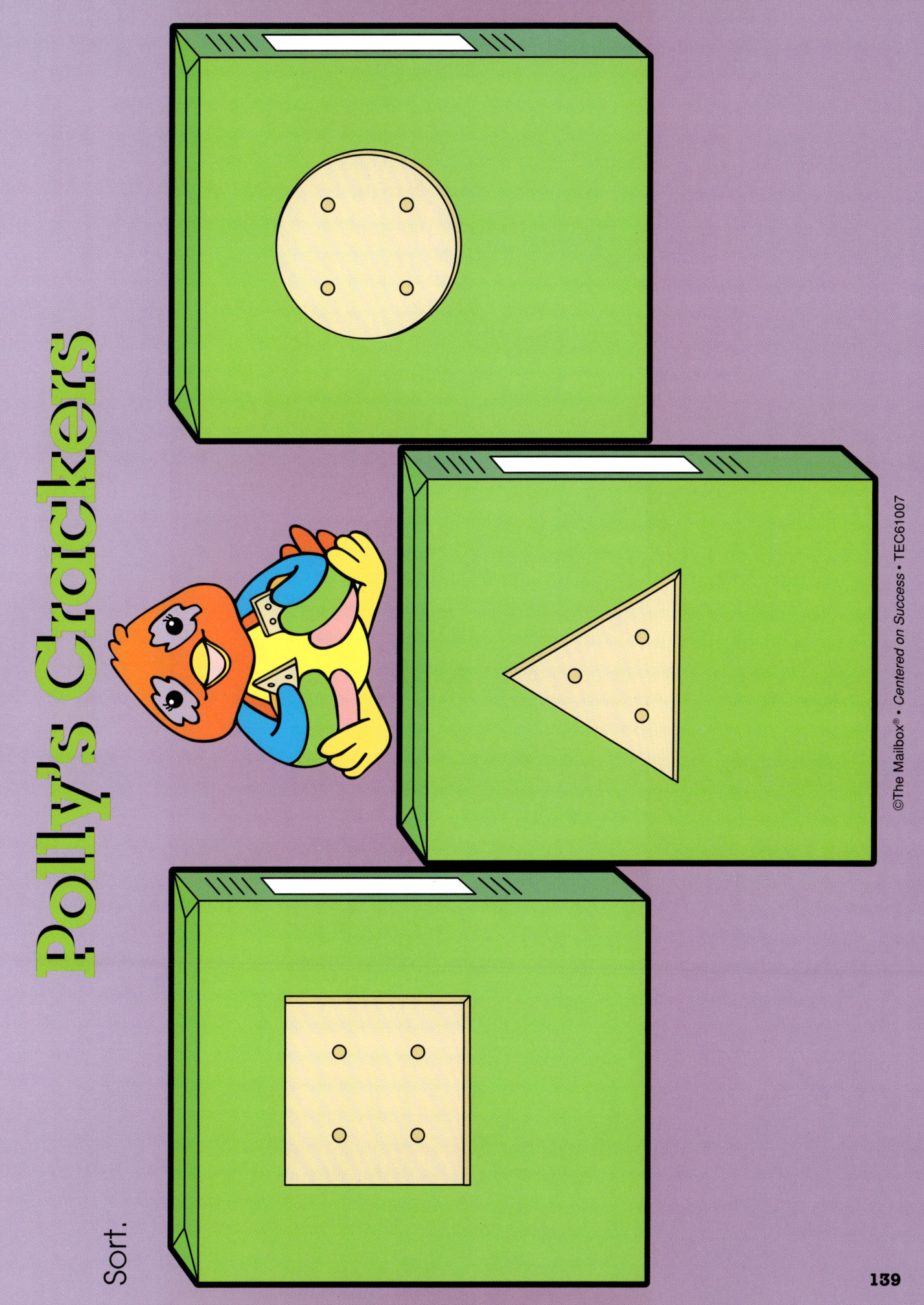

Activity Cards

Use with the directions on page 137.

©The Mailbox® • *Centered on Success* • TEC61007

Activity Cards

Use with the directions on page 137.

143

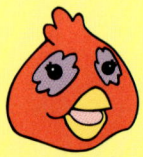 

Activity Cards

Use with the directions on page 137.

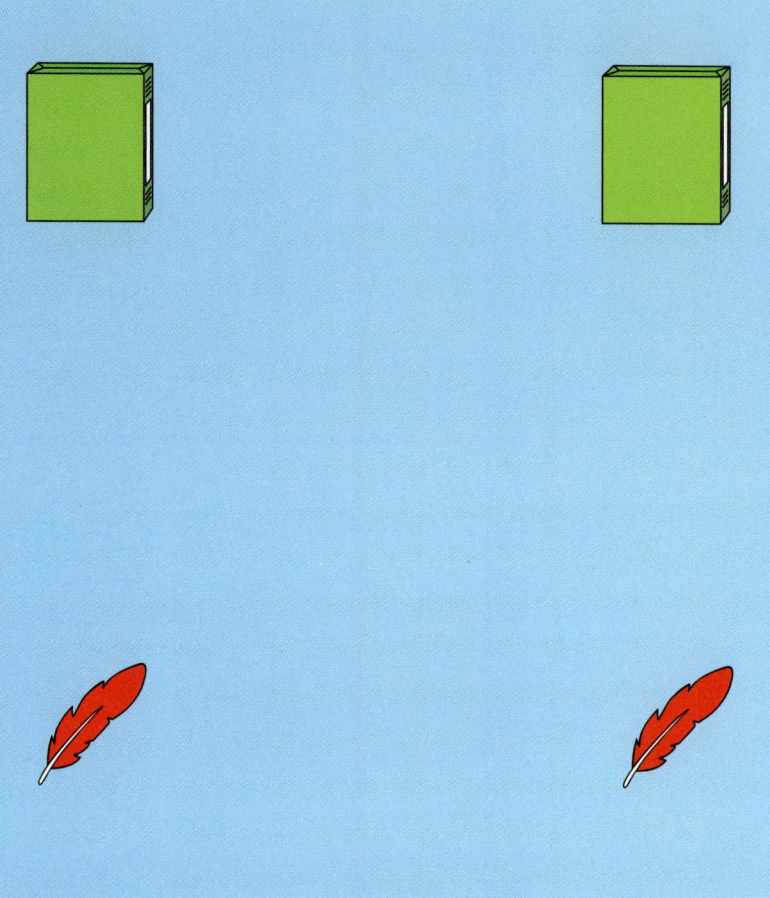

Activity Cards

Use with the directions on page 137.

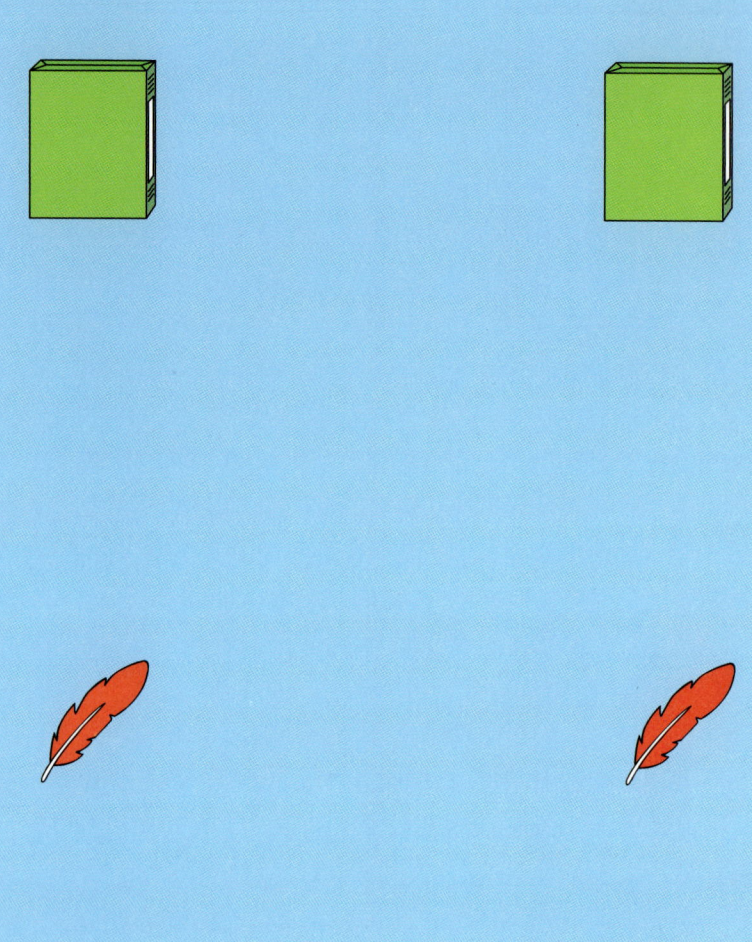

Up, Up, and Away!

 Recognizing pictures that illustrate the position word *above*

 Recognizing pictures that illustrate the position word *below*

Materials:
- center mat on page 151
- 🟡 activity cards and cow pattern on page 153
- 🔵 activity cards and cow pattern on page 155
- 2 resealable plastic bags

Preparing the centers:
Laminate the center mat, cards, and cow patterns if desired. Cut out the patterns and cards. Then put each set in a separate bag. Place the bags and center mat at a center.

Using the centers:
1. A child removes the cow pattern from the bag. She places the cow on the yellow star on the mat if she's completing the yellow center, or on the blue star if she's completing the blue center. She places all the cards faceup in the center area.
2. She chooses a card. She identifies whether the animal pictured on the card is in the same position as the cow on the mat. If it is, she places the card on the mat. If it isn't, she places the card in a separate pile.
3. She repeats Step 2 for each remaining card.
4. She flips over both sets of cards. If the pictures on each set match, she is finished. If the pictures do not match, she rearranges the cards until they are placed accurately.

For Added Fun
🟡 🔵 Transform a variety of animal cutouts into stick puppets, including a cow cutout. Also make a moon stick puppet. Then place all the puppets at your puppet center. Encourage students to visit the center and make up stories about animals jumping over the moon.

Dear Family,
   We have been learning to recognize pictures that show the positions *above* and *below*. Help your child follow the directions shown.

Point to the cow that is *above* the moon.

Point to the cow that is *below* the moon.

● **Cow Pattern and Activity Cards**
Use with the directions on page 149.

  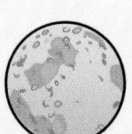

○ **Cow Pattern and Activity Cards**
Use with the directions on page 149.

Here a Chick, There a Chick

 Counting to 5

 Identifying numerals, counting to 10

Materials:
- center mat on page 159
- activity cards on page 161
- activity cards on pages 163, 165, and 167
- 2 resealable plastic bags

Preparing the centers:
Laminate the center mat and cards if desired. Cut the cards apart and put each set in a separate bag. Then place the bags and center mat at a center.

Using the centers:
1. A child removes the cards from the bag and places each one faceup in the center area.
2. If he's completing the yellow center, he counts the chicks as he places them on the nest. If he's completing the blue center, he sorts the numeral cards from the chick cards; then he chooses a numeral and names it. He counts the corresponding number of chicks and places them on the nest. Then he removes the chicks and repeats the process with each remaining numeral.

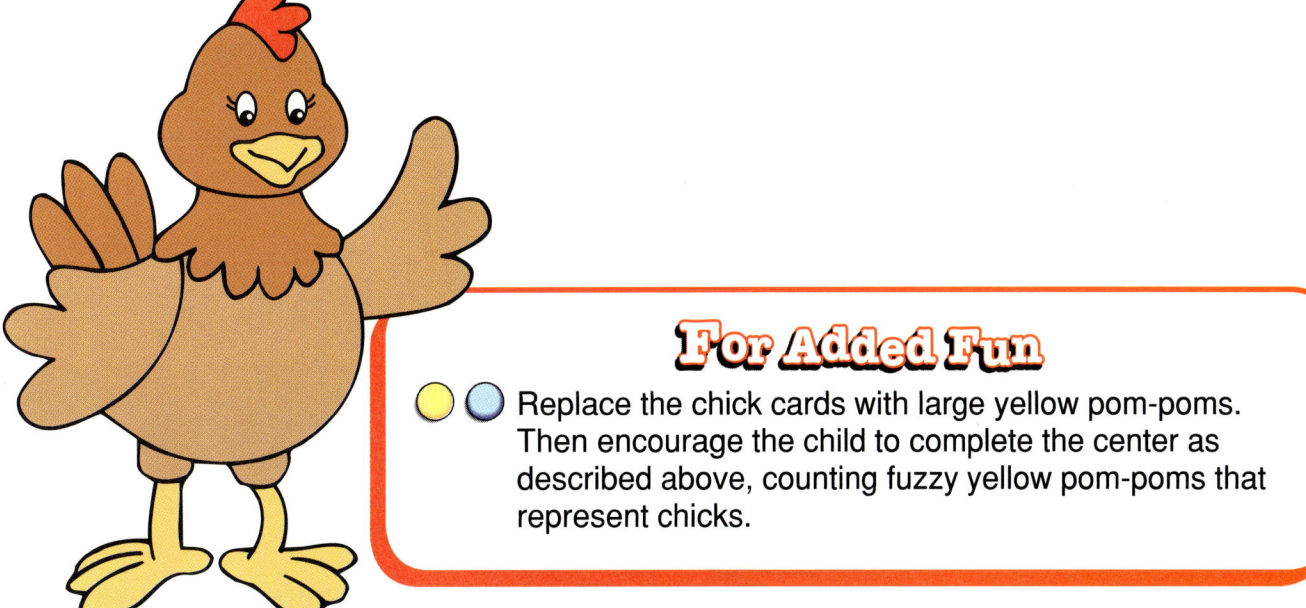

For Added Fun
Replace the chick cards with large yellow pom-poms. Then encourage the child to complete the center as described above, counting fuzzy yellow pom-poms that represent chicks.

Here a Chick, There a Chick

Count.
Place.

Activity Cards

Use with the directions on page 157.

◯ **Activity Cards**
Use with the directions on page 157.

◯ **Activity Cards**
Use with the directions on page 157.

1	2
3	4
5	

Activity Cards
Use with the directions on page 157.

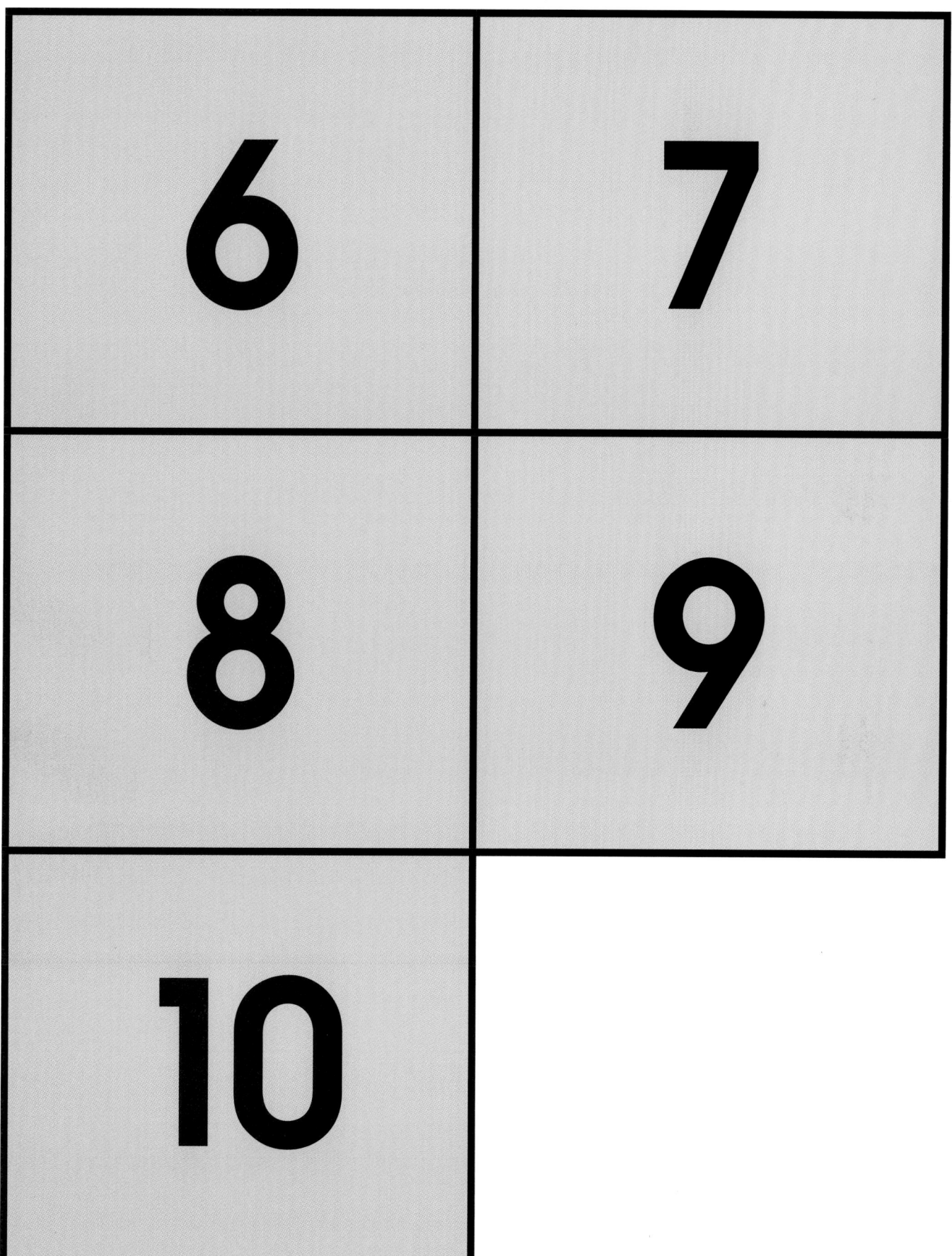